Trading Days

by Rachel Kranz
illustrated by Deborah Colvin Borgo

Chapters

Orlando Boston Dallas Chicago San Diego

Visit *The Learning Site!*
www.harcourtschool.com

For over 10,000 years, the Wampanoag have lived near the Atlantic Ocean. Their name means "People of the First Light," or "People of the Dawn." *Wompag* means "bright light." They took this name because they lived where they could see the sun rise on the ocean.

After the Europeans arrived in North America, the number of Wampanoag people became very small. Today, however, there are five Wampanoag communities in Massachusetts and Rhode Island.

Life in Wampanoag Country

Before the 1600s, when Europeans came to North America, the Wampanoag were known by the names of their communities, such as Nauset, Pokanoket, and Pawtuxet. The Europeans later took some of these names for their own towns.

The Wampanoag believed that land should be for the entire community to use. Each year, the *sachem*, or leader, and the council of elders decided where families could plant, hunt, and fish.

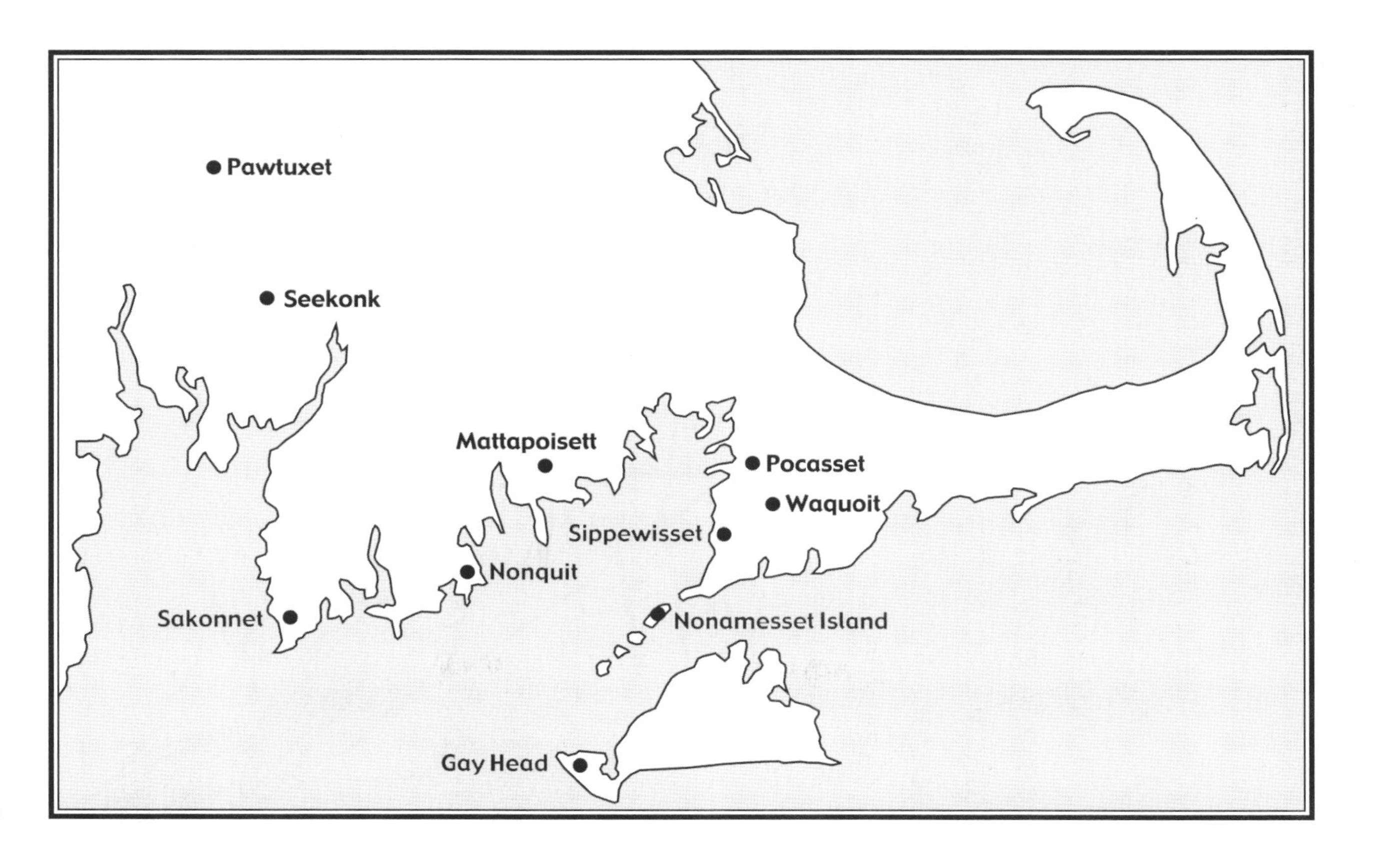

Pawtuxet
Seekonk
Mattapoisett
Pocasset
Waquoit
Sippewisset
Nonquit
Sakonnet
Nonamesset Island
Gay Head

Very long ago, the Wampanoag were hunters and gatherers. Women gathered shellfish, nuts, roots, and berries. Men hunted birds and deer in the winter and caught fish in spring and summer.

About 1,500 years ago, the Wampanoag began to grow crops for food. A Wampanoag story tells about how they began. According to the story, "Our winged relative, the Crow, brought the corn and bean seeds from the lands in the southwest."

The Wampanoag did not have schools. Instead, children worked beside the grownups. Girls learned how to grow crops, grind corn, and cook. They made baskets, pots, and clothes. Boys learned to hunt, fish, and help with crops and cooking.

The Wampanoag helped their children grow to be strong. They knew that girls had heavy work to do. Women would break new ground, plant seeds, weed, and harvest crops. Boys had to be strong, too. They might have to run for miles while hunting or go without food until they caught something.

The Wampanoag also taught their children how to make tools. They made bows, arrows, and spears for hunting. They made nets for fishing. They sharpened rocks for carving and made pointed sticks for planting. They wove baskets for storing food. They made sewing kits and sewed clothes out of animal furs and skins.

Finally, children were taught how to live in a community. Children and elders, men and women, sick and well—all had to work together and support one another.

Each year, the Wampanoag moved several times. During planting and harvest time, they stayed near their crops. When they needed to catch more fish, they lived near the ocean.

Moving day meant lots of work for everybody. During the summer, women dried the food they had grown. They preserved the meat from the animals the men had hunted. At summer's end, they packed the food into the baskets they had woven. Women and girls had heavy loads to carry!

When the people moved, they had to build new houses. Usually a family would live in a "round house." This kind of house was made of bent cedar poles tied together and put into the ground. The poles were covered with mats woven from cattails. Cattails are reeds that grow in marshes.

The warriors had the biggest houses. Their houses had two fires. Their houses were also made of cedar poles, but the poles were covered with bark sheets instead of reed mats.

Most families lived in round houses.
Warriors and other important people lived in bigger houses with two fires.

clay pots – for cooking

bowls, spoons, and ladles – for eating

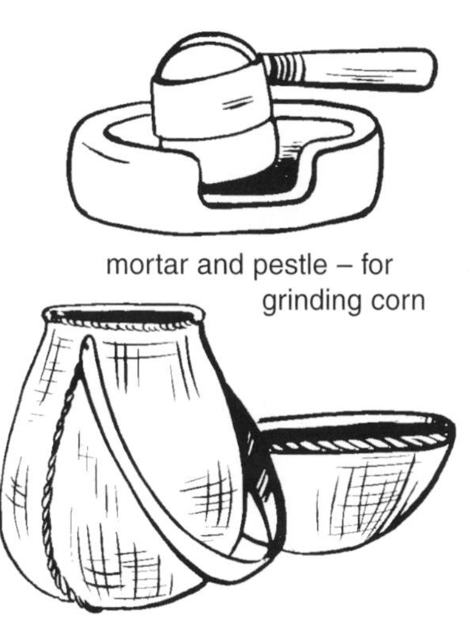

mortar and pestle – for grinding corn

baskets woven out of grass – for storing food

Time to Trade!

The Wampanoag were a resourceful people. They could make or grow almost everything they needed. On special days they exchanged things with other Native American people.

The Wampanoag used *quahog*, a hard-shelled clam, to make jewelry and beads. The shell was broken, and the purple part was carved into beads. These beads were called *wampum*. They were so beautiful that they became well known to all the Native American people.

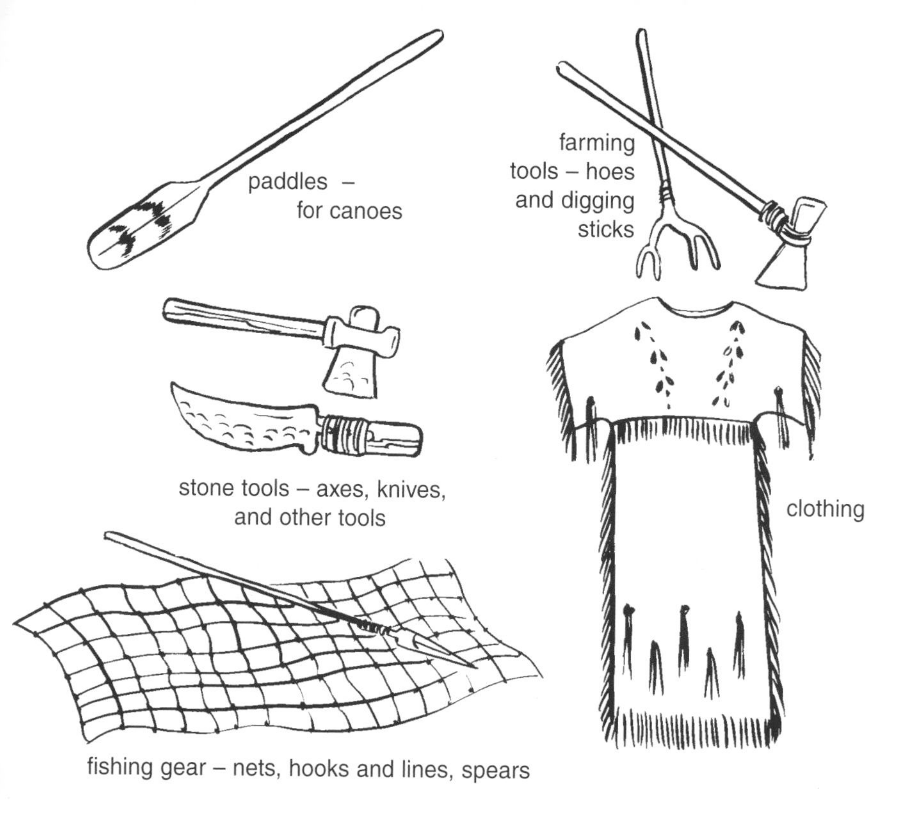

Wampum beads were made into belts and necklaces. They were very valuable gifts. Later, they were also used like money for trading.

About 400 years ago, Europeans started coming to North America on small sailing ships. The Europeans began trading with the Wampanoag and with other Native Americans.

The Europeans needed food. They hunted for some of it. However, they also needed to learn to grow crops.

The Europeans brought metal tools such as fish hooks, knives, and kettles. The Native Americans liked metal because it does not break. The Europeans traded metal objects for food. Trading a strong copper kettle for food or animal furs was considered a good bargain.

After the Europeans came, the Wampanoag still used their own tools. However, they also made good use of the tools the Europeans traded. The metal tools made many difficult jobs easier for the Wampanoag. A Wampanoag who had a machete, or large, heavy knife, could harvest crops much more quickly than before. In 1620, a schooner, or ship, called the *Mayflower* landed at what is now called Plymouth, Massachusetts. On board were people we now call Pilgrims.

The Pilgrims sailed from England. They were looking for a land where they could be free.

The Pilgrims did not know how to survive on this new continent. They were cold, hungry, and in need of help. They had arrived in winter in a place where winters are very cold. The Wampanoag saw how troubled the Pilgrims were. The people of Pokanoket village helped the Pilgrims.

Half of the Pilgrims died that first winter. In the spring, the Wampanoag taught the Pilgrims the best ways to grow food.

The Wampanoag showed the Pilgrims how to grow corn, squash, and beans. They taught them when to plant the crops and when to harvest them. The next winter would not be so hard. Thanks to the Wampanoag, the Pilgrims would have food.

Many people know about the "First Thanksgiving," in which Wampanoag and Pilgrims gave thanks and celebrated their friendship. For a while, the two peoples continued to trade.

Friend or Foe?

Sometimes the Wampanoag and the English acted like friends. They traded goods and gave gifts. At other times, they were enemies.

In time, the English believed that they had bought all the Wampanoag land. The Wampanoag did not agree with that idea at all. They thought that they had agreed to allow the English only to *use* some of their land. To the Wampanoag, people could use land—but no one could own land. Land was for everyone.

Today, the Wampanoag are trying to preserve their old communities. They welcome help from friends of all nations.